I0487516

DID YOU SAY

MARKETING DIGITAL?

PAULA SILVA SANTOS

ISBN-13: 978-1500871307
ISBN-10: 1500871303

DEDICATION

This book is dedicated and designed to assist and facilitate the perception of businessmen and technical marketing in the difficult task of choosing the best tools for the dissemination of their business.

PAULA SILVA SANTOS

CONTENTS

ACKNOWLEDGMENTS

This book is designed to assist and facilitate the perception of businessmen and technical marketing in the difficult task of choosing the best tools for the dissemination of their business.

.

1 - SOCIOLOGICAL ANALYSE

THE HABITS OF THE PEOPLE IN OUR DAY:

2 WHERE IS MY TARGET? HOW CAN I GET THEM?

We know that around the world people spend a significant amount of time on social networks, on average each person spends at least about 120 minutes per day;

Some spend many hours a week;

With iphones truth is the large majority of people only disconnect to sleep!

Now comes the 1st question!

How to get the attention of the huge amount of customers and what tools to use?

We all know that social networks and search engines are the most important tool for the dissemination of a brand, product or service.

The benefits are huge, on one hand we have the release of our "target" and second hand the creation of data bases of qualified customers, who managed effectively, can turn your audience into loyal customers, and this course will be reflected in increased sales.

Now we come across so with the 2nd and 3rd issues.

How can we put these tools working for us?

If we know how, what's the best bet?

I will answer these questions, right now!

3 MODERN MARKETING CYCLE

We know that the Cycle of Social Media works differently compared to traditional means.

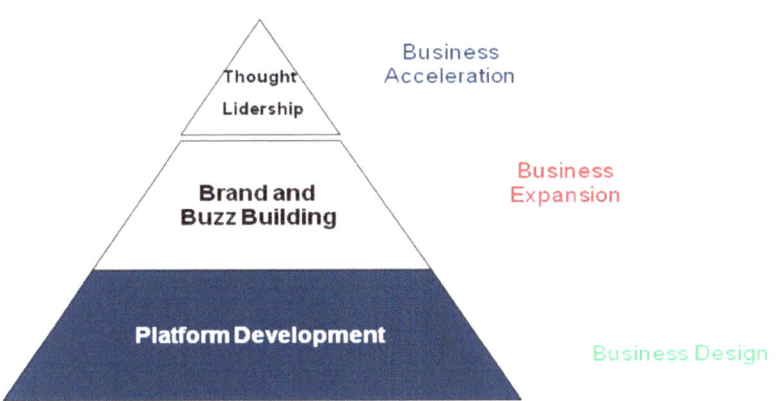

MODERN MARKETING CYCLE

• No one doubts that the key to success in dissemination and recognition of a brand by consumers, and therefore increased sales is the way bet and manages the information of our brand.

I developed various tactics and methods to interact with the public, involving brands and target, provoking:

• Curiosity;
• Interest;
• Necessity to know more about everybody knows…
• And virality

This Book is thus through good communication of your products and / or services through the Social networks a journalistic communication activity that will get your pick if you want to give more visibility to your brand, feel completely freely to contact us by email: webusiness.geral@gmail.com

4 CONVERT TRAFIC INTO SALES

These tools along with appropriate promotional campaigns led their customers where you want ... directing traffic to their blogs / websites / landing pages and sales and in turn will create a larger audience, until it can be viral.

Sounds simple?
But the whole process is a bit more complicated...
Some facts about driving traffic from social medium and convert them into sales can be very surprising:

- 82% of marketers say they use social networking to find clients;
- 62% want to reach customers where they spend their time;
- 56% say that customers expect in social networks known companies and their products;
- 79% of marketers measure the traffic from the social media site, and the metrics of belonging;
- 57% of companies say that sales generated through their blogs;

7

- 48% of companies have generated customers via Twitter;
- 42% through Facebook;
- Search (paid and organic)

5 NEWSLETTER'S

Have Newsletters matter to ensure the maintenance of contacts already qualified and belong to our database.

It is vitally important that the site be friendly to the search engines for easy SEO, also a good brand image.

IN FACT ALL THE TOOLS LEAD TO A HIGHER RATE OF CLICKS (PPC).

And the list is endless …

6 SOCIAL MEDIAS NUMBERS

Knowing the Social Medias generate traffic to where you want, and that can be converted into sales we still see the numbers in another way:

Facebook

1.25 billion Facebook users and 49% of people say that Facebook has great impact on their purchase decision;

Twitter

550 million + users; 34% of marketers say they have gained customers through Twitter and 50% of people are likely to buy the brands they follow;

Google +

+ 600 million users; The (+) button is shared over 4 billion times a day and 40% of marketers use this platform to find customers;

Youtube

Do you know that Youtube displays more than 7 billion video hour per month?

Linkedin

Has 218 + million users; 87% of whom are business executives have a profile on this platform.

Pinterest

Pinterest Has 68 million users; About 78% of this number are women (which is who makes most of the purchasing decisions).

Yes, all these statistics are numbing … and correspond to a sea of… opportunities never seen before.

- ✓ Come to the main part of the way to drive traffic to your websites / blogs and gain new customers with tips thesis you will be an expert in no time!

- ✓ Before we take you to these ways of driving traffic to their huge selling points, just go to the main thesis-rating Interact with their customers on social media is very important, since they are your future customers, and you have to outline its strategy, otherwise it will end up as a lost person in the woods.

- ✓ Leveraging social media platforms and providing your customers may not be on the same platform, it is important to create a campaign for the different platforms, and so your image will be consistent in bringing the public recognition of its brand image, which whatever you are.

- ✓ If your website / page is optimized for mobile phones, 85% of your audience uses phones to shop and seek advice from social media before making a purchase, we cannot ignore this.

7 ANALYSE OF SOCIAL MEDIA ONE-BY-ONE

8 FACEBOOK

So let s start now!

It is one of the most popular platforms, which gives companies the possibility to pre-select your audience in order to reach customers based on widely varying parameters namely:

• Age;
• Geographical location;
• Gender;
• Marital status;
• Academics level;
• Devices

and more interesting is that the Facebook allows you to target your ads based on interests, and advertising spreads at pre-selected friends and also for the public audience, since the news feed makes this spread.

There are also some very interesting ways to reach the audience on facebook here are some:

Contests and giveaways:

This strategy always gets very excited users, first is by GAIN something and on the other hand the leadership that will get.

Thus increases the followers and in turn, leads to greater involvement of the public.

Pages:

There are so many brands on Facebook, how can you stand out?

You should choose very well the content of your page, it is important for users to obtain valuable information about your product and. But you should use your page to also comment on general issues related to journalistic, creative way of general interest and thus create closeness with his audience.

Example: a brand of wedding dresses creates **"insights"** about which there was a parade in Paris and the latest trends in wedding ceremonies and so presents arguments for engaging users in the **subject**, causing them to comment and share, thus generating a *Viral Communication* and **without costs.**

Reward your followers:

Do some action "prize" for their faithful followers, make them feel privileged and appreciated, become more personalized relationship to them, like, share or comment. Will create a chain reaction and increase visitors to your site.

Do not ignore any comments:

Receive feedback whether good or bad, always helps the brand to reflect on where to improve or continue to be better! It is also a golden opportunity to give credibility and highlight the "ignorant" brands. So never ignore any feedback and is always ready to respond and provide solutions. Answers should be given in a time-averaged between 2-6 hours.

Ads:

Facebook ads have great potential, not only to maintain good relationships with existing customers as to build new relationships. Test with ads that can direct to demographics that match your product and so adapted the shopping experience for new users and existing users you can direct them to newsletter's and keep them abreast of news from your company.

AND CONSEQUENTLY GENERATE MORE SALES.

9 TWITTER

Feels that these 140 characters restrict their communication? It really forces us to

be very direct. And Twitter is also known to connect amazing people online. Yes, you can too, I will tell you exactly how!

Twitter lists:

The effectiveness of a list depends on how you use it, basically a list of twitter is like as a hashtag (#) is to mark tweets the same way from a list that person to score. Based on your product and target customer segment, the list of people who can be your potential customers.

Try to engage with at least 5 of them daily, and try to interact with everyone on your list in at least weekly. Retweet, "favorites" and mention are great ways to engage with your prospects, the more people get to be, the more you can the chance.

Target achieved.

Since August the Twitter platform allows more data.

The statistics allow you to track various components of the activity of its Twitter ads, learn more about the behavior of their customers and adjust your campaign for best results.

Observe in real time the performance of your Tweets, Promoted Accounts and Affairs.

It's simple…You will see the fundamental measures of their campaigns Tweets, Promoted Accounts and Subjects, including impressions, retweets, clicks, responses and followers, when they happen.

History is on your side.

The panel's historical activity provides a comprehensive view of all your activities on Twitter. See the performance of each Tweet, with mentions, followers, range and more. So look perceptions, trends and opportunities for optimization.

This is true with the search option that you can learn a lot about your brand, competitors and customers!

With this information, you can keep an eye out for what competitors are doing and compare it with your brand, you can check out what customers are saying by searching and finding the good or bad job and then on this feedback.

The important thing here is to do, look at all that your competitors are not active, and create a search using them to any of these twitter tools. Have you ever committed users are talking about competing theses and there are chances that they will agree with you too.

10 GOOGLE +

 Many traders do not pay attention and have unrealistic expectations from this particular social networking site.

It's time to make Google+ a priority, It is because the platform has some unbelievable skills.

When they say Social Media helps SEO, be sure to use Google+

.

In your circles:

To create a business page Google+ all who have good links to happy / sites-have blogs and a lookout on what users are responding to-and have that incorporated into your strategy. Engage in discussions with, tender and leverage Hangout Where option live stream video with 10 people and other people can see it well, Malthus reach a wider audience.

Google authorship:

Have you ever wondered that when you search for someone and their faces appear? Well, I know the secret to this; They do this by binding and then adding "Google Authorship" to one of the links. So how does that help? You can start by checking your e-mail with Google, then providing a picture of you, you are there strange more "legitimate" now.

Communities

Google communities are a year old and already have over **100,000** Communities.

Communities are as a group or pages for what is so special about them? Messages Google+ 1 can receive from other members and can be re-shared or circles to the communities it reaches a wider audience. You can edit the post anytime. Everything you share with the community also put on the public page. And things that you know should happy to be viable and interesting that attracts new customers.

11 PINTEREST

 Ignoring Pinterest is say NO to their customers. Are you wondering why? Most users on Pinterest are women between 24-44 parentheses, it is that all groups that controls maximum purchase decision. Now I am sure that I have your attention.

Easy Searching:

This is truly de-cluttering with the option to seek their pines. So, it gives you an option to find your pins gold pin re-public, you've stumbled across a very inspiring campaign you had re-arrested, do not stress over it now has been easy for you to search!

Shared plates:

This is a great way to keep a personal relationship with customers in any way, for sharing your stories with pictures as they say a picture is worth a thousand words. So in this particular aspect that you can create a frame and add people as taxpayers and in turn they can add taxpayers making very interactive and a good way to stay in touch with potential customers.

Spell details:

Images that have very vague information is only for those who spell detail is required.
Example:
If you stuck up a product that says all good for gifting customers, now that is very vague. It should be mentioned that the thesis customers are profitable and gifts under 1000 /—can be used for any genre and then provide a link for the same.

12 LINKEDIN

DOES YOUR COMPANY SELL TO OTHER COMPANIES? LOOKING FOR CLUES?

There are more business on LinkedIn They're currently playing. Here is how you can expand the network you are making new connections!

Developing Connections:

The rules are pretty clear on LinkedIn; you can add connections you know. Purpose we are looking to expand our connections, how do we do this? By first completing your profile 100 percent, not only professional details Adding goal to make it interesting too. So when you send a connection with someone you do not know your profile is the first impression for you.

Get introduced:

So let's say you want to add someone to your connection Everything is a profile of a person you know, you can do so by clicking Close in "have introduced", which is on the passenger side of the profile so that you can be accepted, does sour the subject line is intriguing, be specific, introducing yourself as well as graceful and make a request to be accepted ...

Join groups and discussions:

You can build influential relationships, if done the right way. Example: Participate in a group that has a few hundred members and comment on the most popular topic with some interesting insights and be active 2-3 times a week. A well versed start a conversation instead ask a series of questions, though-provoking and if you really get involved with people you "Top influence of the Week", which comes in sets of lateral and then securely attached bar, you can start their own group.

Ways to Increase Sales through Social Media via Digital Insights
(http://webusiness1.wordpress.com)

KEY MEASURES important to remember

The same argument some very important All that are fundamental questions arise for you to remember. Whether one is human social. This is key points you should always remember, never be like a fire hose links, do not make the mistake of just links broadcasting.

> **Be Happy! All that is personal share is Engaging and tastes, actions or responses.**

Be human and not a "robot"! Example: Automatically never send a thank you message or mass; This makes it less personal sccm to be social and send a personal message shows that you care!

Keywords

Know your:. If you want your page to pop up falling on searches, which remain under all keywords matching your products, customers and competitors so odd, so you can enjoy all on social networks.

Hashtags (#):

#Hashtags are a feature used by most social networks, they are used before the word or phrase as # SocialMedia in a way to track and categorize trending topic Everything that is or you want to search, you will see the importance of this on Twitter, Google+, Facebook, Instagram, Pinterest, Tumblr and Vine.

With this you can add to your daily post not just randomly thesis with some relevant and make a good research of what's being said about your brand..

Call to Action: All descriptions that have "Call to Action" to see year increase 80% in engagement.

The testimonials are great as they add credibility to your brand, time to dig deep into your post all the positive feedback and incorporate it into your site, make a list of testimonials and share on other platforms too.

A happy customer leads to another potential

customer!

Thesis with insights into social media marketing, everything is modern marketing mix you can increase traffic to your website and gain new customers.

These are some ideas that I use, and they have worked well for many companies.

If you have any questions regarding this Book or you want to Strategic Social Media Marketing You can contact me at: webusiness.geral@gmail.com

ABOUT THE AUTHOR

Paula has been working in Digital Marketing for the past 15 years, with extensive work experience in the promotion of brands and online business developing.

She is also a certified by Google Ads and Facebook advertising.

Over the past 15 years Paula has developed some business areas for several years for her own company (Multibrand, Lda), always with the use of electronic commerce and the success was due to the ever Digital Marketing tools used to achieve excellent sales results, and Brands knowledge as this business cause, were always ONLINE.

Paula has been a consultant to various companies in implementing Digital Marketing strategies.

In training activities taught by Paula Silva Santos, are supported by some case-studies of real brands.

Paula Silva Santos, has special pride in offering the best techniques, the result of about 15 years of study and constant updates, as well as the latest tools available across platforms.

Her career spanned both the technical and business aspects of digital marketing, which means that she is able to fill the gap between the two and make better use of the tools and technologies available.